A special gift for

_____

with love

_____

date

_____

Stories, sayings, and scriptures to Encourage and Inspire

hugs™

for
Chocolate
Lovers

~MMY BICKET
~D DAWN BRANDON

~rsonalized Scriptures by
ANN WEISS

HOWARD BOOKS
A DIVISION OF SIMON & SCHUSTER
New York   London   Toronto   Sydney

Our purpose at Howard Books is to:
•*Increase faith* in the hearts of growing Christians
•*Inspire holiness* in the lives of believers
•*Instill hope* in the hearts of struggling people everywhere
Because He's coming again!

Published by Howard Books, a division of Simon & Schuster
1230 Avenue of the Americas, New York, NY 10020
www.howardpublishing.com

HOWARD
BOOKS   *Hugs for Chocolate Lovers* © 2006 Howard Books

Library of Congress Cataloging-in-Publication Data
Brandon, Dawn M.
  Hugs for chocolate lovers : stories, sayings, and scriptures to encourage and inspire / Dawn Brandon and Tammy Bicket.
    p. cm.
    10 Digit ISBN: 1-58229-483-6; 13 Digit ISBN: 978-1-58229-483-4
    10 Digit ISBN: 1-4165-3394-X; 13 Digit ISBN: 978-1-4165-3394-8
    I. Christian life—Miscellanea. 2. Chocolate—Miscellanea. I. Bicket, Tammy L. II Title.

BV4515.3.B73 2005
158.1'28—dc22

2005052823

10 9 8 7 6 5 4 3

Manufactured in the United States of America

For information regarding special discounts for bulk purchases, please contact Simon & Schuster Special Sales at 1-800-456-6798 or business@simonandschuster.com.

Paraphrased scriptures © 2006 LeAnn Weiss,
3006 Brandywine Dr., Orlando FL 32806; 407-898-4410

Cover design by Stephanie Walker
Interior design by Tennille Paden

Scripture quotations are taken from *The Message*. Copyright © 1993, 1994, 1995, 1996, 2000, 2001, 2002. Used by permission of NavPress Publishing Group. Information about chocolate, its health benefits, and historical facts were gleaned from a compilation of widely published studies and historical data.

Contents

In the sweetness
of friendship let
there be laughter
and sharing of
pleasures.

Kahlil Gibran

Chocolate Holidays

Just as you suspected, chocolate lovers—there's at least one reason a month to go hog wild and celebrate chocolate!

January 3—National Chocolate-Covered Cherry Day

February 19—Chocolate Mint Day

March (third week)—American Chocolate Week

April 21—National Chocolate-Covered Cashews Day

May 15—National Chocolate Chip Day

June 16—Fudge Day

July 28—National Milk Chocolate Day

August 10—S'mores Day

September 13—International Chocolate Day

September 22—National White Chocolate Day

October 28—National Chocolate Day

November 7—National Bittersweet Chocolate with Almonds Day

December 16—National Chocolate-Covered Anything Day

Chapter 1
Sweet Rewards

$\mathcal{R}$emember that every good
and perfect gift is from Me.
My law is more rewarding than
fine gold. You'll benefit from
demonstrating kindness to
others. When you give, I give
back to you much more than
you've given.

Rewarding you,
Your Gracious Heavenly Father
  —from James 1:17; Psalm 119:27;
  Proverbs 11:17; Luke 6:38

Anyone who has ever given a young child chocolate ice cream in a hot car on a summer day knows that you often get back much of what you give. The same goes for giving chocolate to a dog (strongly discouraged for so many reasons). Receiving back when you give might not always be pleasant, but it can be—when you give the right stuff, under the right circumstances, in the right way.

In the positive sense, some people see this principle of return as being "You scratch my back and I'll scratch yours." But that's shortsighted and limiting. The higher ideal is that loving service to others naturally results in benefits to us as well. Like when we bake chocolate brownies at a child's special request. We do it for the child, but we, too, get to enjoy the smell of them while they're baking, and we get to sample them. By the same principle, when we help a friend stick with her diet, we almost always lose a few pounds ourselves. When a mother puts her child's needs ahead of her own, she sacrifices some things but gains some intangibles that are far grander— self-respect, discipline, love, and the joy of giving.

When our motive for kindness or giving is a reward, we're bound to be disappointed. But when we give from a generous heart, with love and compassion for others, we just can't help having some of the sweet stuff come back to bless our own lives.

All love is sweet,
given or returned.

Percy Bysshe Shelley

Carly lifted the pillow she'd been holding over her face. Couldn't she have a little time for herself one day a year?

Icing on the Cake

"Mommeeeee . . ." Ben's voice came from the hall outside Carly's bedroom. "Can we make cupcakes now?"

Carly lifted the pillow she'd been holding over her face, trying to keep this day from beginning, and cleared her throat as quietly as she could to steady her voice. "I'll be there in a minute, honey. Why don't you watch cartoons while I get dressed?"

"I guess."

Carly could hear the disheartened tone in her six-year-old's voice and his shuffle back toward the living room. She knew he had wanted to make cupcakes for his Sunday school class, but why did it have to be *today*? And why on earth did it have to be the first thing she did? Couldn't she have a little time for herself one day a year?!

"Chocolate, Mommy—they have to be chocolate, with chocolate icing," Ben had demanded. He'd definitely inherited his mother and grandmother's taste for chocolate. Carly could almost taste the homemade, buttery, chocolate frosting her mother used to pile on top of rich, dark chocolate cake.

She rolled onto her side and stared at the framed photo of her mother. *You always made my birthday special. You made everything OK. I wish you were here.* Fresh, hot tears started to flow. So many things had changed over the past couple of years since her divorce, including her mother's death eight months ago, that Carly could barely catch her breath, much less buoy herself up and put on a cheerful face. She always did her best for Ben's sake, but some days life was almost more than she could bear.

Oh, she could brave the big things—being solely responsible for Ben, working full time, trying to take care of the tiny, older house she'd bought with her small inheritance. Oddly enough, it was the little things that seemed most difficult—like not getting a birthday cake on her birthday. *That's silly*, she'd tried to tell herself. But her heart wasn't listening.

Little knuckles were tapping on her door. "Mom?"

Carly pushed back the covers. "Coming, sweetie." She threw on a pair of beat-up, comfortable jeans and a gray sweatshirt, then pulled her hair up into a ponytail. *One thing about motherhood, your self-pity sessions have to be brief. Or at least carried on without your kids' knowing about them.*

She went to the kitchen and poured chocolate-hazelnut coffee beans into the grinder. At least she'd treat herself to her favorite gourmet brew. It'd been months since she felt she could splurge on the expensive beans. Lately she'd had to settle for whatever coffee was on sale at the grocery store. She pushed the button, and the grinder ground—to a halt.

"You've got to be kidding me," Carly muttered. *I can't even have a nice cup of chocolate coffee on my birthday?* The tone in her head crescendoed toward an all-out wail, she felt her throat tighten, and she was just about to lock herself in the pantry for a good cry. She knew there was still one box of tissues in there.

But she heard the commercial break begin on TV, and sure enough, around the corner came Ben, ready to "help" bake cupcakes. Carly gritted her teeth to try to keep her lips from quivering. She reached into the cupboard for the can of sale-brand coffee grounds.

"OK, babe, find the mix in the pantry, and I'll help you get out the ingredients." Ben's whole face lit up with a wide grin. He pulled his special stool over to the shelf and selected the darkest chocolate Duncan Hines mix from amid the other three cheaper chocolate-cake mixes.

Oh, great, Carly thought. *My favorite kind finally goes on sale, and now I have to give it away to a bunch of kids.* But she was too embarrassed by her selfishness to object.

"How was school yesterday?" Carly asked as she pulled eggs from the fridge. She had worked the late shift at the hospital the previous night, so the sitter, Penney, had tucked Ben into bed.

"OK."

"Just OK?"

"Yeah."

Ben had seemed a little evasive about school lately, but when Carly talked with his teachers, they all vowed he was doing great and interacting well.

"Did you get your chocolate milk?" she prodded. Each afternoon the kids could buy snacks from a snack cart. She'd tried to encourage Ben to choose apples, but it was no use. He was his mother's son. He wanted Hershey bars. They had compromised on chocolate milk. At least that had *some* nutritional value.

"Yeah. Billy splashed his all over his face and clothes, though, when he tried to prove he could poke the straw through the carton without opening it. It was all in his hair too," he said with a giggle.

Carly couldn't help but smile. This was more like her usually chatty son. She sent him back to the pantry for some vegetable oil while she got out the hand mixer that had been her mother's. *How many cakes did Mom and I make together with this?*

"Mom, can we still have my next birthday party at Grandma's house?"

Carly's stomach turned to lead as she remembered the downside of that chattiness. Ben asked a lot of questions—questions about things Carly had tried to explain but somehow, apparently, failed.

"No, honey. Grandma's in heaven now, remember? And we don't live in that house anymore." Living with her mother after the divorce had felt like such a refuge. The monetary savings really helped, and her mom had been great about helping with Ben. But the thing Carly had needed and appreciated most during that time was someone to make her feel special. Her mom always seemed to know how to do that. Now Carly felt rootless and adrift.

Ben's question conjured up images of her own childhood birthdays in that house. The memories simultaneously beckoned to her like an oasis and haunted her like a tormenting ghost. *I miss being the kid. I miss someone doing things for me!*

Ben emerged from the pantry. "Can I put the stuff in the bowl?"

"Sure." She helped him combine the ingredients, then she put her hand over his as they whipped the batter . . . *of a cake that I'm making for someone else on my birthday!* She felt the resentment welling up again. She'd considered buying herself a birthday cake, but that seemed kind of pathetic, and besides, now she'd have to put the quarters she'd been saving in her jar toward a new coffee grinder. *And I just refuse to make my own birthday cake!*

"Mom, you're squeezing too hard!"

Carly realized she had a death grip on the mixer, smashing poor Ben's little hand. She fought back tears again. "Oh, sweetie, I'm sorry. Mommy was thinking of something else, and I didn't realize. Come on, let's pour the batter into the cups."

After the cupcake pan was placed in the oven, Ben disappeared into his room while Carly cleaned batter and its various ingredient remains off the counter, then poured some coffee and sat down to sulk over the newspaper. *I can't even get a cup of coffee until after ten o'clock because I'm making chocolate cupcakes, my favorite kind, on my birthday, for someone else's party!*

OK, Carly, let it go, she rebuked herself. *You're being ridiculous. Grow up. This is for Ben and his friends, remember?*

I'm tired of being grown up. I want to sit down and cry! I want something—anything—to be about me and not about bills or laundry or driving a carpool!

She let out a soft groan to drown out the dueling voices in her head and went to retrieve the cupcakes from the oven and let them cool. Then she made her mother's famous frosting and put it in the fridge so it would retain that amazing fluffiness until she was ready for it.

"Ben, I'm going to jump in the shower, then we'll ice the cupcakes after I'm done," she called to him through his closed door.

"OK," was the muffled reply.

Carly sighed. *You could say, "Happy birthday, Mom!" Or, "I love you, you're a great mom, thanks for doing all this stuff for me even though this day is supposed to be about you!"* She clapped her hand hard to her forehead as she closed her own door. *Carly! He's six!*

After an inordinately long shower with the small consolation of a chocolate-hazelnut-scented candle, Carly emerged feeling somewhat calmer, if resigned and still sad. She knocked on Ben's closed door. "OK, kiddo, I'm ready."

Icing on the Cake

He answered from the kitchen. "Out here, Mom!"

Carly's thin veneer of composure nearly shattered when she rounded the corner. Ben had decided to frost the cupcakes himself, and the results were everywhere—on the counter, on the floor, on his shirt, in his hair—she didn't know how any of it had landed on the cupcakes. But then she saw the proud look on Ben's face, and her frustration and self-pity melted faster than ice cream under hot fudge. He was beaming. Smudged, but beaming. Suddenly it was easy for this to not be about her.

"Wow, honey, you did it all by yourself!"

"Wait!" Ben ran back to his room, and Carly tried not to wonder whether he was tracking chocolate frosting on the carpet. He returned with his hands behind his back.

"Happy Birthday!" he squealed as he presented a giant-sized chocolate bar and a handmade, construction-paper card. "To Mommy," it read in uneven letters. "Your the best mom evre, and I love you. Happy Birthday."

Carly tried to gulp down the huge lump in her throat. "Oh, sweetheart, it's beautiful, thank you so much! But where did you get the candy bar?"

"Penney helped me. I saved up all my chocolate-milk money, and she took me to the store last night."

"But honey, you love your chocolate milk!"

Ben played it cool. "It's OK, Mommy." He marched over to the kitchen counter and handed her a cupcake. "These are for you too. I just pretended about taking them to church. I wanted to make you a cake like Grandma used to, but I didn't

know how to do it by myself. You always do nice stuff for me. I wanted you to feel special."

Carly covered her mouth to stifle a sob, but the tears wouldn't be held back. She gave Ben a big hug, and he kissed her cheek.

"Thanks, baby. You've made this the best birthday Mommy's ever had."

She released him, sniffled, and grabbed a few tissues from the pantry. "Now let's eat cake!"

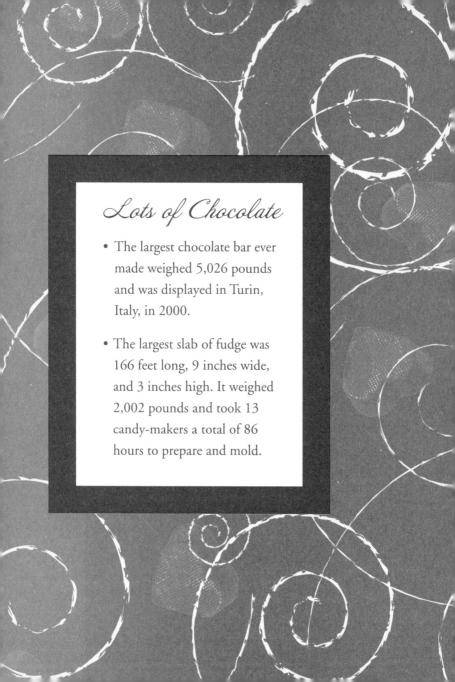

Lots of Chocolate

- The largest chocolate bar ever made weighed 5,026 pounds and was displayed in Turin, Italy, in 2000.

- The largest slab of fudge was 166 feet long, 9 inches wide, and 3 inches high. It weighed 2,002 pounds and took 13 candy-makers a total of 86 hours to prepare and mold.

Chapter 2
Sweet Investment

$\mathcal{M}$y words are sweeter than honey to your mouth. Don't lose heart in doing good. Look for opportunities to invest in others. Encourage people daily and build them up. You'll see rewards if you don't give up.

Filling your heart,
Your Faithful Provider
   —from Psalm 119:103; Galatians 6:9–10;
   Hebrews 3:13; 1 Thessalonians 5:11;
   Proverbs 28:10

On his last voyage to the new world, Christopher Columbus became the first European to encounter chocolate. In commandeering a loaded canoe off the coast of what is today Honduras, Columbus's son, Fernando, noted how highly the local people valued its cargo of an unusual "nut" he and his father had never seen before. After bringing the cargo and some islanders onto the ship, Fernando noticed that whenever one of these "nuts" fell, the islanders scrambled to retrieve it. What the Europeans thought were strange almonds were actually cacao (or cocoa) beans—prized locally as money.

Although the Columbuses undoubtedly took some of this treasure back to Spain, no one in the Old World recognized the value of chocolate for another twenty years.

It's hard for modern chocolate lovers to understand how anyone could fail to appreciate chocolate's appeal. But in its raw form, chocolate isn't so appealing. The precious treasure hides deep within fibrous pulp, in a coarse, green pod. In the natural, even its bittersweet flavor might not appeal to Western tastes. But processing makes all the difference.

Anything worthwhile requires something of us—an investment of time, effort, or resources. Sometimes it's hard to invest in people. We can't control their responses, change comes slowly, and we aren't guaranteed any return. But people are the sweetest kind of investment with the greatest potential. Don't be guilty of writing off people as "nuts." They might actually be chocolate beans.

Always serve too much hot-fudge sauce on hot-fudge sundaes. It makes people overjoyed and puts them in your debt.

Judith Olney

*No wedding,
no shower—no gift.
It's just not fair!*

The Sweet Shoppe

The new girl definitely was not endearing herself to anyone. As a matter of fact, she was practically asking to be smacked, Christine decided. Whitley was tall and blond, with a body straight from Hollywood and teeth Christine was sure could light up the entire chocolate shop during a power outage.

"Hi, Teeny. Comin' to my weddin'?" Whitley's voice dripped honey as she breezed by, waving her wedding invitation so no one would miss it.

Oh yeah, then there was that syrupy southern accent straight from *Designing Women*. Christine added another fault to Whitley's sizable list. Everyone seemed to fall all over themselves wanting to hear dear, sweet Whitley talk. Like they'd never heard anyone from Georgiabamalina—or wherever she was from—talk before.

And this "Teeny" thing just proved how unclever Whitley was. Did she really think it was the first time anyone had ever thought of altering Christine's name to draw attention to her slight, five-foot-nothing

frame? She'd been called Teeny ever since second grade—which was just about the level of sophistication Whitley displayed by calling her that. So what if most people still called her by that nickname. It somehow sounded worse when Whitley said it.

"Is it OK if I post this invitation on the bulletin board?" Whitley asked, pausing with a flourish beside Barbara Boston, the store's co-owner and general manager. "I don't want anyone to miss it. Y'all are invited."

"Go ahead, dear," Barbara responded kindly. "I'm so happy for you! And I hope you'll allow Barb and Bev's Sweet Shoppe to provide the wedding cake and sweet treats for the reception—a gift for you and your husband-to-be."

"Well, isn't that wonderful?" Whitley gushed, then disappeared into the back room momentarily.

"Isn't that wonderful?" Christine mocked quietly, exaggerating Whitley's accent and fru-fru hand gestures.

"Christine!" Barbara shot her a look that somehow managed to communicate both a warning and understanding. *She* always managed to get the name right.

"Thanks for giving me the week off," Whitley said, reemerging. "You know how many details there are to attend to before a big weddin'—oops, I guess neither of you gals *would* know," she giggled. "Sorry!"

Christine was speechless with anger. She was sorry Whitley was too far away to smack and too oblivious to notice Christine's glare that could have vaporized chocolate.

Whitley opened the door but stopped and turned before

leaving. "Oh, don't forget my shower tomorrow night, gals. I'm registered at Saks if anyone's still wondering what to get." With that and a dramatic wave of her hand, Whitley was gone.

But her presence lingered. "Can you believe that?" Christine fumed. "If she thinks I'm *ever* going to buy her a present or go to her stupid *weddin'*, she's even more delusional than I thought!"

"Christine," Barbara soothed gently. "Don't let anyone ruin your day or change your sweet, generous nature."

Sweet? Generous? Christine had never heard anyone apply those words to her before. Some of her anger deflated as she considered Barbara's words.

"Come on." Barbara locked the door behind Whitley and turned the sign in the window to read Closed. "We have a lot to do if we want to get out of here at a decent hour. We have fifty pounds of chocolates to wrap and package for that special order tomorrow."

Christine sighed and headed for the candy-cooling tables in back. Wrapping chocolates could be tedious, but sampling was always fun. Besides, she had no reason to hurry home. Whitley was right. It wasn't like she had a husband—or even a date—to hurry home for. Still, the indignation and anger at Whitley continued to burn as she wrapped chocolates quickly and efficiently.

"So are you going to Whitley's shower and wedding?" Christine demanded to know when Barbara joined her.

"I am," Barb replied cheerfully. Christine realized that

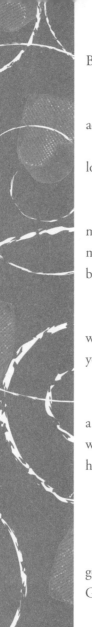

Barbara was softly humming the "Wedding March."

"And you're really donating the wedding cake?"

"And chocolates and pastries for the reception," Barbara added.

"She's taking advantage of you," Christine protested. "How long has she worked here, three months?"

"Just two," Barbara corrected.

"Guess it just seems longer with Whitley," Christine mumbled. "Is she going to keep working here after she's married, or is she just getting a free cake and lots of extra gifts before running out on us?"

"She hasn't mentioned quitting."

"They never do before the wedding." Christine might as well have just said *duh!* "You know this always happens, don't you?"

"What always happens, dear?" Barbara asked nonchalantly.

"It's like a revolving door here," Christine said, plopping a slightly misshapen chocolate into her mouth. "That one wouldn't have reflected well on Barb and Bev's," she explained, her mouth full.

Barbara smiled. "Thanks for protecting my reputation."

"They're using you."

"Who's using me?"

"Is there a sign down at the college that says 'Planning to get married or have a baby? Save yourself a bundle of money. Get a job—briefly—at Barb and Bev's Sweet Shoppe.'"

Barbara laughed. "We do seem to have a lot of weddings

and births around here, don't we? That's one of those things that goes along with working with young people."

"How many of these things do you go to every year?" Christine pushed. "How many gifts are you expected to buy for others?"

"I've never counted," Barbara admitted. "But I suppose it's quite a few."

"And how many gifts have you gotten in return? None! No wedding, no shower—no gift. It's just not fair!" Christine continued her rant, not noticing that Barbara had stopped wrapping chocolates and was silently watching her. "At least married women can't complain. I can't imagine they ever shell out for as many gifts as they receive at their weddings—and then at multiple baby showers. But single women like us get burned every time. We're expected to give, give, give . . . smile, smile, smile."

"Christine," Barbara protested. "Giving gifts isn't an obligation. It's an opportunity to invest."

"In what, someone else's silver collection?" Christine countered.

"In someone else's life—in their future."

"But most of these people just breeze in, pick up their gifts, and breeze back out, never to be seen again," Christine protested. "It's not right for them to expect gifts from us."

"It's not right to expect gifts," Barbara said thoughtfully. "But it's always right to give them." Christine glowered in skepticism as Barbara continued. "Investing in people is like

investing in anything. You don't always get a return, but when you do, it's worth far more than you've invested."

"How is it ever worth it?" Christine demanded.

"Well, for one thing, when I had my surgery last year, a lot of those people you accused of disappearing came through for me. I heard from a lawyer in Denver, a missionary in Guam, a grandmother in Tampa, a teacher in Memphis, and at least a dozen people from across the state—all former employees in whom I'd invested long ago."

Christine plopped another chocolate into her mouth and laughed bitterly. "It still doesn't seem worth it to me—giving and giving on the chance that someday, someone might come through. I don't want to invest. I'm swearing off showers and weddings—beginning with Whitley's."

They finished wrapping the chocolates. Christine waited for Barbara to close up the back of the shop so they could walk together to their cars.

"I know Whitley has gotten on your bad side," Barbara brought the subject up again as they walked across the parking lot. "But don't let her turn you against weddings—or people in general." She stopped walking, turned to face Christine, and placed a hand on her shoulder. "Choosing to give isn't about the one who receives as much as it is about you. Giving blesses the one who gives."

Christine couldn't suppress a snort of disbelief. "I guess I'm willing to sacrifice that particular blessing."

"Christine, I've gone to a lot of weddings and showers over the years and given lots of gifts, but I don't regret a single one. In fact, my only regrets have come from not going or giving."

"You mean there was a wedding or shower you actually skipped?"

Barbara nodded her head solemnly. "Quite a few. I once felt much as you do."

"You're serious?" Christine asked, intrigued. "What changed?"

"I was young. I'd been working in a little chocolate shop downtown. I'd probably been to a dozen weddings in as many months, and I was tired of it. So when a new gal started work just a month before her wedding, I didn't feel obligated to go. I figured she didn't know me well enough to miss me, and I'd never know her well enough to care."

"And?"

"She's been my best friend for thirty years. And I deeply regret having turned down the opportunity to share the most special day in her life."

"You mean Bev?" Christine's eyes narrowed in surprise.

Barbara nodded. "That experience taught me that I couldn't know what life would bring or what stranger might end up being the most important person in my life. It just seems smart to treat every person as a dear friend you just haven't gotten to know yet."

"I guess I do know Whitley—too well."

"We all learn life's lessons in our own time, dear," Barbara said kindly. "You're a smart girl—a good girl. I know you'll learn what's important—in time."

I can't believe I'm doing this, Christine thought as she slid into the pew beside Barbara, Bev, and several other gals from the Sweet Shoppe. She was encouraged by Barbara's warm smile.

"I'm proud of you, dear," Barbara whispered to Christine as the organ music swelled for the start of the processional. "I hope you didn't feel pressured to come."

Christine chuckled. "A little," she admitted. "But no one could force me if I didn't want to."

"I know," Barbara's eyes twinkled. "So why did you come?"

"I guess I didn't want to someday regret having missed sharing a special day with a special friend." She looked at Barbara meaningfully.

Barbara smiled as she wiped away a tear. "Don't mind me," she said. "I'm just a sucker for weddings."

The Milky Way

- Sixty-five percent of Americans prefer milk chocolate to dark.

- Chocolate makers in the United States use about 3.5 million pounds of whole milk daily. They use 40 percent of the almonds and 25 percent of the peanuts produced domestically.

- One ounce of milk chocolate has caffeine roughly equal to a cup of decaffeinated coffee. You'd have to eat about eight 3.5-ounce bars of milk chocolate to consume the amount of caffeine you'd drink in a regular cup of coffee. So skip the coffee and hit the chocolate!

Chapter 3
Sweet Compromise

*K*eep a discerning heart and listening ears. My wisdom is a sweet fountain of life to your soul, and My words will give you light and understanding. Bear with one another. You'll find that true love supersedes a multitude of faults.

Uniting you,
Your God of Peace
　　—from Proverbs 18:15; 13:14;
　　Psalm 119:130; Colossians 3:13;
　　1 Peter 4:8

Whether it's politically correct or not, what you always knew deep down is true: there really are big differences between men and women. Scientific studies have determined that while men most often report craving spicy foods, like pizza, women overwhelmingly report chocolate as their strongest, most common craving. The scientists also assure us, however, that craving chocolate has less to do with some chemical addiction than with the pleasing taste and texture of chocolate.

Is it any wonder there's conflict when people can't agree on something so basic and important as whether they like chocolate? Thankfully, the power of compromise is stronger than all our differences. Centuries ago the

Aztecs loved a drink that was both spicy and chocolaty. Some chocolate makers today have learned a lesson from the past. Hot, new chocolate flavors include chili, curry, and cayenne pepper.

While some things are too important to compromise—our morals, our self-respect, the truth —most of the things that cause conflict with others are far less important than our relationships with those people. Rather than clinging stubbornly to "my way" and rejecting "your way," we can talk through things and embrace new ground in the middle: "our way." Not only does compromise draw us closer to those we love, it also opens our eyes to new tastes and knowledge. We just might discover we like spicy after all.

Only when we experience
love can we experience
life to the fullest.

Ida Fay Oglesby

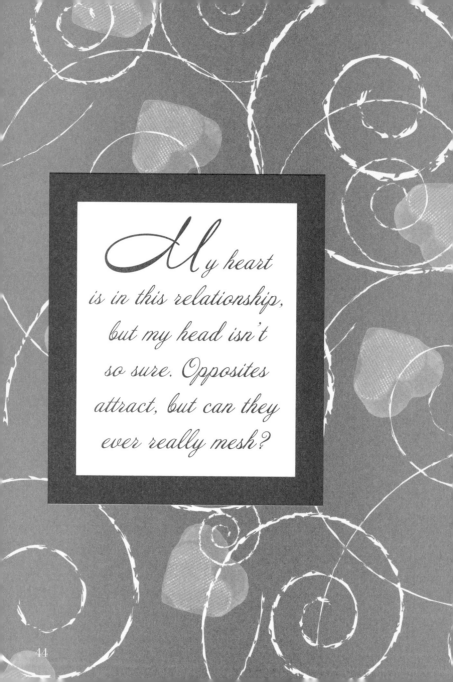

My heart is in this relationship, but my head isn't so sure. Opposites attract, but can they ever really mesh?

Milk Chocolate

"How about this one?" Lauren held up a classic black dress.

Jen was already ten steps ahead of her, heading toward the casual-wear department. "Uh . . . he's taking me to a farm show."

Lauren stared at her incredulously and spoke slowly. "Your date is a farm show."

Jen laughed. "Yeah. Dairy cows. Can you believe it?"

"Wow. You must *really* like this guy. You don't even like milk."

Jen gave her friend a hesitant look. "I do . . . like him, I mean . . . but I'm thinking of breaking up with him."

"What?! Jen, when did you start thinking of breaking up? I was just joking around—I know you really like Brandon. I thought he might be the one! Does he know this is coming?"

"No! You're the only person I've said anything to." Jen shoved the blouse she'd been holding back onto the crowded rack, then raised her arms and let them fall in exasperation. "Lauren, I don't know what to do. My heart is in this relationship, but my head isn't so sure."

Lauren blew out a long, slow breath. "OK, what's holding you back?"

"Well, in case you hadn't noticed, we're pretty different."

Lauren laughed and raised her eyebrows. "That you are. But opposites attract, right?"

"Oh, they attract. But can they ever really mesh? I mean, my mom and dad love each other, in their own way, but let's face it—they take separate vacations! She reads, he fishes. She travels around the world, he's never left the state. They go to different restaurants for dinner, for crying out loud! Different is not necessarily good."

Lauren motioned with her hand for Jen to lower her voice. "OK, so maybe you have a point."

Jen realized she was attracting attention and let out a quiet groan. "Oh, come on, let's go. I'm not in the mood to shop anymore anyway."

"You? Not in the mood to shop? This is serious." They headed back out through the mall, toward the exit.

"OK, let's think this through. So you're different. That doesn't necessarily mean you'll end up like your parents, right?" Lauren turned around to hold the door open for Jen. "I mean, you fell head over heels for this guy. *Something* must have attracted you to him. Besides the fact that he's *totally* hot—and seems, from my perspective, totally into you—what do you like about him?"

Milk Chocolate

Jen gave a sly smile. "Well, being good-looking does *not* hurt."

She sighed and looked toward the sky, slouching her shoulders just a little as they walked toward their apartment complex nearby. "I don't know. I mean, there are a lot of good things. He listens—how many guys really listen? But what if he's just being nice now, and he'll get tired of listening to things he really has no interest in, and five years from now I'll be chattering away to the back of a newspaper!"

"Whoa, whoa, whoa. First, nobody said you had to marry the guy tomorrow—or ever. One step at a time. Second, this is the good list, remember? We can deal with what-ifs later."

Jen rolled her eyes. "OK. Well, he's kind and fun. Did I tell you we took my nieces and nephews to his dad's farm? Brandon took them all on tractor rides, taught them how to milk a cow, and let them climb the bales of hay. They had a blast!"

"Well, see, that's a good quality—a guy who can relate to kids can't be all bad."

"But Lauren! There were *bales* of *hay*!" She held out her hands, palms up. "*Cows*, and bales of hay! I felt like I'd stepped into another world. I don't know anything about that kind of life. I go to art museums and poetry readings!"

Lauren was laughing so hard she could hardly get the key into the lock on the apartment door. Jen couldn't help but giggle too.

"Oh, wait, I haven't told you the best part. He was actually wearing *overalls*!"

Lauren turned around as if to be sure Jen was serious. Then she half-snorted. "Really?"

Jen grinned. "Although, I hate to admit, he made even those look awfully good."

"OK." Lauren plopped on the couch. "So we can live with the overalls. What else?"

"Well . . ." Jen stared out the window. "He's thoughtful. I don't mean just considerate, although he is. I mean he really thinks about stuff. He's smart." She paused and grabbed a chocolate from the bowl she always kept filled on the coffee table.

"And he's content. I know that sounds weird, but there's something kind of appealing about that. It's like I'm always at ease when he's around, ya know?"

"Hmm. Sounds pretty good to me. Are you sure you wanna break up with this guy? And can I have him?"

"Noooooooo!" Jen wailed, squeezing her eyes shut and putting her free hand on her head. When she opened her eyes again, she saw Lauren's look of surprise. "Oh—I mean, no, I'm not sure at all that I want to break up with him."

She shook her head and tried to explain. "It's just that all the things that seem good on one hand seem to promise trouble on the other."

"Huh?"

"OK, look. He's considerate, but sometimes to the point of not speaking his mind, whereas I think everything should be brought out into the open. He thinks about stuff, but not about any of the same kinds of things *I* think about. Our talents don't cross paths at all. And he's content—but does that mean he'll never want to go anywhere or strive for anything?" She held up the empty candy wrapper and made a display of crumpling it. "He doesn't even like *chocolate*! He orders *fruit* things for *dessert*! Lauren, I could go an entire *month* and not miss eating fruit!"

Lauren was smirking, and Jen could tell her friend was showing great restraint, trying not to laugh at her. She rolled her eyes. "Oh, go ahead," she said, smiling, then started to laugh at herself. "I'm a mess."

Lauren chuckled. "You're going to dump a perfectly great guy because he eats *fruit*?"

Jen tilted her head, smiled, laughed, and then started to cry. Lauren put her hand on her arm.

"Jen, think about it. Do you really want him to be just like you?"

"Well, a little common ground would be nice!" Jen snapped.

"OK." Lauren took on her tough-counselor tone. "So what you want is an argumentative, poetry-writing, world-traveling, art-history major who spends his spare time scrapbooking and yammering on about stuff you already know."

Jen just glared.

"Look," Lauren softened her voice. "There's some common ground, or you wouldn't be together after six months, right? But where's the fun in being exactly alike?"

Jen stared at the wrapper she'd wadded into a tight ball. She

knew her friend was right. "Lauren, what am I going to do?"
Tears burned her eyes and flowed down her cheeks. "I think I
love Brandon, but I'm so afraid that we'll end up like my mom
and dad."

Lauren handed her a tissue and looked Jen in the eye.
"Hon, Brandon is not your dad."

Jen sighed heavily and wiped away tears. She spoke quietly
now. "But he reminds me of my dad, you know? That's both
great and scary. My dad is a *great* guy, and I love him. But
compromise isn't in his vocabulary. He just doesn't give. He
never complains when my mom does her own thing, but he
doesn't join her either. I don't want to live like that."

Lauren was quiet, listening.

Jen sniffled. "I mean, I'm sure my mom must've thought he'd
change some, you know? That they'd both adapt." She dabbed at
her eyes with another tissue. "How can I know if Brandon will
meet me halfway or just insist on doing things his way?"

The doorbell rang and Jen jumped up in a panic. "Yikes!"
she whispered. "That's him! I didn't realize what time it was!"

"OK, OK, shh . . . go fix your face. I'll keep him busy
talking about . . ." she shrugged and gave Jen a questioning
look. "Pasteurization?"

Jen shot her friend an exasperated look, then smiled and ran
to her room.

She emerged ten minutes later, hoping the cold-water splash
and concealer hid the splotches under her eyes.

"Hey," she greeted Brandon as cheerily as she could. She

still felt torn and uncertain. If only she knew they could meet somewhere in the middle of things. "Ready to go?"

"Yep," Brandon answered as he put his arm around her and kissed the top of her head.

"Oh, here," he said as he handed her a small, unadorned shirt box.

If this is flannel, it's over, Jen thought. What she said was, "Oh, thanks," as she lifted the lid and pulled back the tissue paper concealing what was inside. She froze, mouth hanging open. Inside were at least a dozen huge, chocolate-covered strawberries.

"It's nothing much. I picked them this morning at Dad's and dipped them myself this afternoon so they'd be fresh. I thought maybe if I used lots of chocolate, you wouldn't notice there was fruit inside." Brandon poked her gently with his elbow and gave her that irresistible smile.

She looked up at him, speechless. Lauren peered into the box, smiled, and cleared her throat. "Well, you two have fun," she said, giving Jen a wink, then quickly disappeared into her room.

Jen grinned so wide she thought her face would break. Blinking back fresh tears, she looked into Brandon's eyes and took a deep breath.

"They look fabulous."

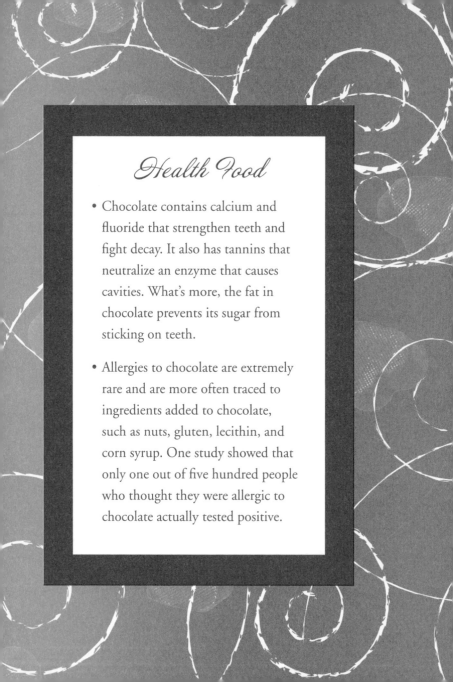

Health Food

- Chocolate contains calcium and fluoride that strengthen teeth and fight decay. It also has tannins that neutralize an enzyme that causes cavities. What's more, the fat in chocolate prevents its sugar from sticking on teeth.

- Allergies to chocolate are extremely rare and are more often traced to ingredients added to chocolate, such as nuts, gluten, lecithin, and corn syrup. One study showed that only one out of five hundred people who thought they were allergic to chocolate actually tested positive.

Chapter 4
Sweet Motivation

$\mathcal{D}$esiring good things will
lead to sweet satisfaction.
May you spur each other on
to love and good deeds. Taste
and experience My absolute
goodness, and know that My
goodness and love will surround
you each and every day.

Thinking sweet thoughts of you,
Your God of Light
   —from Proverbs 13:25;
   Hebrews 10:24; Psalms 34:8; 23:6

One of the greatest sacrifices dieters face is giving up chocolate. Chocolate is high in calories and saturated fat, so no matter how much they adore it, some try to give it up.

But listen up, chocolate lovers: there are many legitimate reasons to make chocolate a part of your healthy, balanced diet. Dark chocolate reduces high blood pressure, protects blood vessels, promotes heart health, and helps prevent some cancers. Plus, chocolate wakes us up and gets us moving. Chocolate lovers know the physical and emotional lift that comes from eating it. Caffeine and other stimulants in chocolate increase the activity of neurotransmitters in the brain, making it easier to pay attention and stay alert.

But perhaps chocolate's best aid to dieters is sweet motivation. As a reward for careful eating, nothing beats chocolate's power to modify behavior. Who can't be good all day when she knows there's chocolate ice cream for dessert? Who wouldn't work out a little longer at the gym in exchange for a square of the rich stuff?

When we desire good things—like chocolate, an education, a strong relationship, or self-improvement—we're much more likely to work hard to achieve them. Working toward good goals and achieving them is sure to bring great satisfaction. What do you desire? How will you reach yourgoals? With hard work and determination—and maybe a little chocolate motivation —you can do it!

A true chocolate lover finds ways to accommodate his passion and make it work with his lifestyle.

Julie Davis

Who ever heard of a diet that lets you eat chocolate?

One Sweet Diet

It was a mystery—a mystery that was practically driving Emmy Bond crazy. Or maybe it was just hunger.

"Where's Trixie?" Emmy's oldest sister, Donna, quizzed her about their middle sister as Emmy slid into the restaurant booth across from her.

"I don't know," Emmy replied, trying to hide her curiosity about the whole situation. "I didn't see her car in the parking lot."

"It's not like her to be late," Donna said, stirring Sweet'n Low into her iced tea with a fat, red straw. "Why didn't she pick you up like she usually does?"

"Who knows?" Emmy shrugged, pulling her purse off her shoulder and stowing it on the seat beside her. "She called yesterday and told me to drive myself. Left a message on my machine saying she'd just meet us here—again. Something's up with that girl." Emmy leaned conspiratorially across the table. "Do you think something's wrong, Donna? Change of life, maybe?"

"Shh," Donna hissed. Her eyes sent a warning Emmy understood instantly.

Sweet Motivation

"You're late." Donna slid over to make room on the seat for Trixie to sit beside her.

"I was here on time," Trixie dismissed the accusation with a wave of her hand as she sat down. "I was in the restroom freshening up a little."

Emmy searched Donna's eyes for some reaction. Neither said anything. They looked away as the waiter came to take Emmy and Trixie's drink orders.

"A Mountain Dew sure is tempting," Emmy said ruefully. She patted her stomach, then closed her menu with resolve. "But I'll be good. Especially with these two watching." She nodded at her sisters. "I'll just have water."

"I'll have the same, and I think we're ready to order." Trixie looked to Donna and Emmy for confirmation.

Emmy could have told the waiter what Donna would order: a half-sized grilled chicken salad with fat-free ranch dressing—on the side, no breadstick. But Emmy was starving. She wanted the twelve-ounce sirloin with sautéed mushrooms, Cheddar potatoes, and garlic bread. But since the sisters' diet pact, she had made it a rule never to order anything that weighed more ounces than the pants size she was trying to fit into—eight.

Who was she kidding? Right now she'd be happy just to fit into a size twelve. She sighed in resignation and ordered the vegetable plate—hold the cheese sauce. With great interest, Emmy waited to hear what Trixie would order.

"I'll take the grilled tilapia with mango salsa and a side of rice," Trixie said, sliding the menu back to the waiter. "And then I'd like the hot-fudge chocolate-brownie cake for dessert." She smiled at the stick-thin young waiter, who nodded and left to place their order. "He's kind of cute," she remarked offhandedly. "But he could use a few more pounds."

"And a few more years," Donna added.

"I'd be more than happy to donate a few of mine," Emmy volunteered. "Pounds *and* years."

Donna turned suddenly toward Trixie. "So you're really serious about this?"

"About the waiter?" Trixie asked innocently. "He's just a little eye candy."

"Not the waiter," Donna waved her off impatiently. "You're serious about this . . . this chocolate *diet* of yours?"

"I'm serious all right," Trixie replied, smoothing her shirt over her waist. "It satisfies the sweet tooth without offending the stomach. What's more, it's really working. I'm down another four pounds, and I have way more energy than I used to."

Emmy eyed Trixie carefully. She had to admit that her sister did look thinner. She could see it clearly in her face: there was more definition in her cheeks and jaw line. She was pretty sure her sister's sporty warm-up suit was new as well, a good indication that Trixie had dropped another size. *But there's no such thing as a chocolate diet! How is she doing it?*

"I refuse to believe a chocolate diet can work." Donna was

clearly exasperated. "It's counterintuitive. That dessert you ordered must have seven hundred calories. You can't lose weight with a diet that allows for that every day. It's just not possible!"

Trixie's eyes danced mischievously. "If it's not possible, how do you explain my losing twenty-five pounds in just over two months?"

"I don't know," Donna admitted, looking miserable. "I can't. All I know is that I've been religiously counting calories and cutting out fat. I haven't had even a taste of chocolate in months—yet I've only lost nine and a half pounds."

"And your sense of humor," Emmy teased. "Relax, Donna, it's nothing personal. We're both a little grumpy since we started dieting. You have to admit your calorie counting makes you a little uptight. I never see you without your little calorie book. I, on the other hand, dream constantly about carbs— pasta, bread, mashed potatoes, French fries, ice cream . . . hot fudge chocolate brownie cake . . ." Her words trailed off as she imagined the taste and texture of her forbidden tempters.

"You're the one who chose low carb," Donna scolded. "You thought it would be easier than the sensible low-fat, low-cal diet I chose."

"It seemed pretty sensible compared to Trixie's chocolate diet," Emmy defended her decision. "Who ever heard of a diet that lets you eat chocolate? Are you really eating chocolate every day, Trix?"

"I swear." Trixie raised her hand as if taking an oath.

"And you're not starving yourself the rest of the day?" Emmy probed.

"I haven't missed a single meal."

"Are you being careful to eat a balanced diet?" Donna pushed. "Getting enough dairy, fiber, fruits and veggies?"

"Oh yes," Trixie promised.

The conversation halted as the waiter brought their food. He accidentally placed Trixie's fish in front of Emmy, and she fought a sudden urge to grab the garlic toast. But Trixie seemed to read her mind and quickly exchanged plates.

Emmy didn't even close her eyes or hear the short prayer Trixie said before they ate; she stared hungrily at that bread.

"So what's your secret?" Emmy asked, her eyes following the bread as Trixie raised it to her mouth and took a bite. "How can you eat chocolate every day and still lose weight so easily when it's such a struggle for Donna and me?"

"Losing weight isn't easy for anyone," Trixie admitted. "But think about the psychology of eating. It's as emotional as it is physical. Diets never work if you end up feeling deprived."

"*I* feel deprived," Emmy admitted, grabbing Trixie's bread as soon as she put it down.

"That's why people fall off the wagon." Trixie stared meaningfully at Emmy, whose mouth was full of Trixie's toast.

"Hey, it's bread," Emmy defended herself, a dry crumb shooting indecorously across the table. "It has to be better for me than chocolate!"

Trixie's smile looked genuinely sympathetic. "If we can unravel the mystery of the psychology of dieting, we have a better chance of success."

"Sounds like mumbo jumbo to me," Donna said sullenly, savagely attacking the dry leaves of her salad.

Trixie ignored her. "Chocolate is how I reward myself for being good. And because I love chocolate so much, I'm *very* motivated to be good."

"But hot fudge chocolate brownie cake just has to outweigh any good you can be gaining from doing well on your diet," Emmy insisted, polishing off the last of her steamed broccoli.

"Ah, but you can't overlook the importance of exercise," Trixie said.

"Well, that explains the athletic clothes," Emmy ran her finger across her plate, trying to get every last drop of butter sauce. "You joined a gym!" Trixie shook her head. "Hired a personal trainer?"

"No! I've just been walking more—and drinking more water too." Trixie raised her glass for a refill as a waiter walked by with a pitcher. "Both will speed up your metabolism. Burning more calories means you can eat more."

"But still . . . ," Donna protested. "I just can't believe it. I mean, come on, it's chocolate!"

As if on cue, Trixie's dessert arrived. No one spoke, but all eyes lingered enviously on the luscious-looking treat as Trixie slowly savored every bite.

Emmy realized she was unconsciously licking her lips. *This is torture. I can't watch this.* She stood up abruptly, picked up the check, and headed toward the cashier. "My treat today. Meet me at the door when you're done."

Donna and Trixie joined her a few minutes later, and she followed them outside. Yes, she could tell that both her sisters had lost weight, but Trixie really looked fantastic. Maybe she should quit skipping carbs and start eating chocolate too. That would be one sweet diet.

Outside, Donna turned left and Emmy went the opposite direction.

"I'm parked over here," Donna said.

"I'm this way." Emmy turned to Trixie, who was fumbling in her purse. "Which way are you?"

"I'm going your way."

"Bye, then," Donna said. "You'd better have parked really far away if you're hoping to walk off that chocolate, Trix."

"Oh, I did," Trixie laughed. She and Emmy waved at Donna and headed the other direction.

"Here's my car." Emmy opened her car door.

"See you later, little sis." Trixie put her hand warmly on Emmy's shoulder. "Thanks for lunch."

"You're welcome." Emmy put on her most powerful little-sister pouty face. "You know, you're setting the bar on this diet so high that I'll never be able to live up to your example. You're supposed to help your younger sister succeed, not make her decide it's not even worth trying."

"Is that how you feel?" Trixie seemed surprised.

Emmy nodded piteously, milking the pressure for all it was worth. "Don't you think you should let me in on your secret— and help me learn how to lose weight like you're doing?"

"Seriously, Em. It's all in the walking. I'd be happy to walk with you if you're serious. If you want, I can swing by your place tomorrow, and we can walk together. Would you like that?"

"I sure would!" Emmy beamed. *This is going to be great!* "See you tomorrow." Emmy climbed into her car, then stopped and shouted toward Trixie, who was moving away. "Uh, Trix, where *is* your car?" Emmy asked, curiously.

Trixie's eyes twinkled. "At home, in my garage."

"What?" Emmy gasped, realization slowly dawning. "But that has to be five miles away!"

"If you cut across the park, it's four point two," Trixie corrected, checking something in her hand—a pedometer— which she hooked on her waistband. "And four point two miles home again. More than enough to make up for hot fudge chocolate brownie cake. And if I had known you were paying, I would have gotten it with ice cream!" She laughed. "But don't tell Donna yet, OK? It's kind of fun driving her nuts." And with a wink, Trixie sauntered away.

Chocolate Goes to War

- In 1940 the Mars company first made M&M's to make chocolate more convenient for soldiers. Chocolate was easy to eat even during battle and provided soldiers as much as 1,800 calories per day.

- During the Gulf War in 1992, Hershey worked to make chocolate more heat resistant, producing chocolate bars that resisted melting at temperatures up to 140 degrees Fahrenheit.

Chapter 5
Sweet Consolation

*P*leasant words are sweet to the soul, and sharing them brings healing. When you bless others, I'll also bless you. And no matter what you experience, you don't have to fear; I'm here to comfort you. As you delight yourself in Me, I'll give you the things your heart really longs for. You can trust Me to do far beyond all that you can ask or dream.

My abundant blessings,
Your God of Comfort
   —from Proverbs 16:24; 11:25;
   Psalms 23:4; 37:4; Ephesians 3:20

These days chocolate is being lauded for many newly discovered benefits. Dermatologists have found that applying chocolate topically renews and moisturizes the skin, making us look younger and more beautiful. Scientists are excitedly studying chocolate's ingredient theobromine as a promising cough suppressant that seems to work better than traditional elixirs, without any of the side effects. Perhaps most striking is the discovery that dark chocolate is packed with flavenoids, an antioxidant that protects against cardiovascular disease.

Of course, chocolate lovers have always sworn by chocolate's other benefit to the heart. Women especially turn to chocolate regularly for comfort and consolation. Whether it's the rich, sweet taste or some chemical that influences our emotions, chocolate makes us feel better when we're sad or hurting.

All of us can be like chocolate. We can't moisturize a friend's skin or stop her cough, but we can soothe her heart. We can be a shoulder to cry on, a listening ear, a word of comfort. We don't have to have all the answers. All it takes is a heart that cares and a firm commitment to stay, even when we'd rather run the other way.

Funny thing about being there for someone at her time of greatest need: when we comfort and bless another, we invariably feel blessed and encouraged ourselves. Won't you be chocolate to someone who needs consolation today?

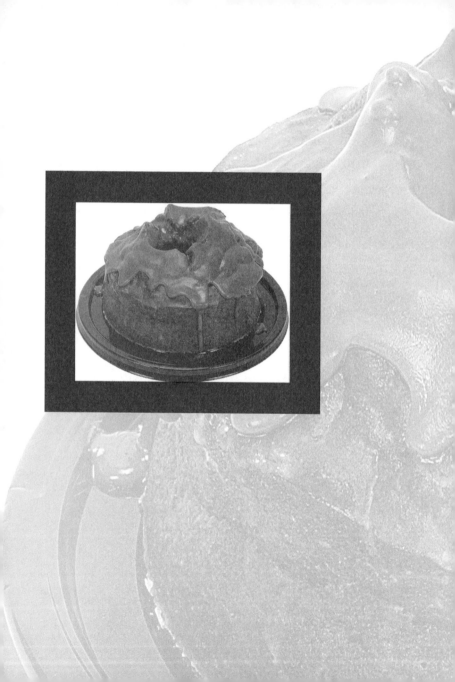

Kindness is more than deeds. It is an attitude, an expression, a look, a touch. It is anything that lifts another person.

C. Neil Strait

It had been two years since her taste buds had savored heaven, and she was determined that nothing—absolutely nothing—was going to keep her from indulging this year.

Chocolate Trifles

M. J. Miller, vice president of textbook sales and distribution, always made good business contacts at the educators' convention in Branson, Missouri. But that's not why Michelle Miller, queen of chocolate lovers, looked forward to coming every year. That honor would fall to the Chocolate Truffle Cheesecake Delight. She had sampled the finest chocolate desserts at the most exclusive restaurants in all of the major metropolitan areas on the continent, but none could top the rich confection served at Top of the Rock in Branson. Contrary to the area's reputation as the hill-billy and country-music capital of the Midwest, the quaint restaurant was set atop a scenic bluff overlooking beautiful Table Rock Lake, and it featured good food and a magnificent view—whatever the season.

But the Chocolate Truffle Cheesecake Delight was so good, it wouldn't have mattered if the dessert had been served on a paper plate with a plastic fork in an un-air-conditioned hole-in-the-wall restaurant in the worst part of town, where patrons had to stand and

listen to the owner's daughter belt out "Stand by Your Man" while they ate. Michelle still would have sought it out each time she was in the area. She had once traveled to Branson after an appointment in Kansas City—a round trip of roughly five hundred miles—just to get a piece of that dessert.

Now she had completed her responsibilities, her bags were packed, and she wasn't due at the airport in Springfield for another eight hours. *Chocolate Truffle Cheesecake Delight, here I come!*

As she slung her purse and cosmetic case over her shoulder, preparing to leave her hotel room, an unbidden thought popped into Michelle's mind. *Call Paula.*

Where had that come from? Paula Arroyo? She hadn't thought of Paula in ages. They'd lost touch a few years out of college as their lives took different paths. She wasn't even sure if her old chum still lived in the area. Curious, she thumbed through the phone book. *What was her husband's name again? Robert? No, Rick.*

She found the number, hesitated only a moment, and then dialed. It was such short notice. What were the odds that Paula would even be home, much less free to meet her for lunch? Part of her hoped there'd be no answer: she almost hung up after five rings. But on the sixth ring, someone picked up.

"Hello?"

The voice sounded odd, not like her friend Paula's animated, happy tone. Michelle fought the urge to say "wrong number" and hang up. "This is Michelle Miller—Michelle Weaver Miller. Is Paula available?"

Chocolate Trifles

There was silence for a moment, then the voice sounded surprised. "Michelle? Is that really you? This is Paula."

"Paula, I'm in town for a convention. I only have a few hours before I head back to the airport, but I was wondering if you'd like to meet me for lunch at Top of the Rock. We could remember old times . . . catch up on what's been going on in each other's lives . . ."

Paula hesitated, and once again Michelle wondered if she'd done the right thing in calling. "I know it's short notice. I'll understand if you have other plans."

"Oh, no, I'm free," Paula reassured her. "I'd love to see you again. But Top of the Rock is a little pricey. Would the diner work just as well for you?"

"I really had my heart set on Top of the Rock," Michelle pressed. Last year when she had tried to make her annual rendezvous with chocolate perfection, the restaurant had been closed because of a kitchen fire. It had been two years since her taste buds had savored heaven, and she was determined that nothing—absolutely nothing—was going to keep her from indulging this year. "It'll be my treat," she promised. "Can you meet me there in an hour?"

Michelle smiled warmly at the woman sitting at her right elbow. "I'd like raspberry tea," she told the waitress who inquired.

"I'll just have water," Paula said. "With lemon."

Michelle glanced at the menu while she tried to think of

something to say after their initial greeting. She was surprised at how much her old friend had changed. Had it been ten years? Twelve? Her hair was shorter. She was startled to notice streaks of gray in the lovely black locks. Paula was a couple of months younger than she was—not yet thirty-five. Her neat clothes were in a style that had been popular several years earlier, and they hung a little too loosely on her thin frame. Although her body was gaunt, her face looked puffy. *Is she sick?* Michelle wondered. Paula looked so much older than Michelle remembered. She wondered if Paula was thinking similar thoughts about her.

"I'll have the small wood-fired vegetarian pizza," Michelle told the waitress when she brought their drinks. "I want to be sure to save room for dessert."

"I'll just have the water," Paula nodded at her glass. "I had a late brunch," she explained at Michelle's quizzical look. "I really couldn't eat." She squeezed a lemon into her water and took a sip. "Oh, I brought you something," she announced, rummaging in her purse. She produced a picture and laid it on the table in front of Michelle. It was a picture from Michelle's twentieth birthday party.

"Oh, I remember this!" Michelle squealed with delight, studying the photo with great interest. "You surprised me," Michelle remembered. "You had a huge chocolate cake decorated at the local bakery to share with all our dorm mates. But it went so fast I didn't get seconds."

"Hey, I had to carry that thing to the dorm on the city

bus," Michelle reminded her. "You're lucky it reached the dorm at all."

What struck Michelle most about the photo was not how young they both were, but rather how sparkly and full of life Paula's eyes had looked back then. It was obvious that something had intervened to change that. Michelle wondered what it was, or what business of hers it was to ask.

"So tell me what's been going on in your life," Michelle pressed gently. "Is everything OK?"

Paula's dark eyes clouded even more. She dropped her gaze, hung her head, and sighed wearily. "Oh . . . a lot's happened in the past few years. I won't depress you with details."

Michelle saw a tear fall into Paula's lap. She pressed a tissue into her hand and lingered there, her own hand on top of Paula's, trying to communicate empathy. "I care about you—and what has happened," she said softly. "I'd be honored if you felt like sharing whatever it is that has wounded you."

Paula squeezed Michelle's hand. It was obvious she was struggling to speak without crying. "It was a year ago today," she started. "Your calling was an answer to prayer . . . I was really at a low point . . . I miss him so much . . . Listen to me. I'm such a mess. You didn't come here to listen to me ramble and feel sorry for myself."

"You let me decide what I came here to do," Michelle gently reprimanded Paula. "Tell me what happened a year ago."

"My six-year-old son, Jake. He had cystic fibrosis. He was sick his whole life, but it got really bad the last couple of years.

It was so hard to take care of him . . . so hard to see his little body fighting for breath. But I didn't want to let him go." The tears flowed freely now, and Michelle moved her chair closer, put her arm around Paula, and hugged her. "I miss him so much, Michelle. I still can't believe he's gone."

"Oh, Paula, I'm so sorry. I'm so sorry I didn't know or help you through this. Please, tell me all about Jake. I want to know everything you loved about him, everything that made him special."

Paula looked up with tears in her eyes, but they shone once again as she spoke of Jake. She showed Michelle a picture and was clearly proud when Michelle noticed how much Jake's nose and smile were like his mother's. They laughed together at the mischief Jake had occasionally caused, marveled at the profound things he'd said while he was dying, and cried about his final hospitalization and struggle to live.

Michelle was grieved to learn that Paula and Rick had had inadequate medical insurance for Jake. Now, on top of the incapacitating sorrow they faced at losing their only child, their financial struggles would be ongoing for many years.

"Let me treat you to dessert," Michelle pressed, when the waitress came by with the dessert menu. "It'll make you feel better."

"They do look fabulous," Paula agreed, studying the tempting photos. "But I can't. Maybe I could just try a bite of whatever it is you're having?"

"Of course!" Michelle promised. "The desserts are huge—

plenty to share." She strongly suspected that Paula was turning down dessert for financial reasons, rather than from lack of hunger. She would gladly have bought Paula the moon just then, but she wanted to be careful not to offend her sense of self-respect.

Paula tapped one of the dessert photos. "On Jake's last birthday, we celebrated here. He was terribly sick. I guess we kind of knew it might be his last, and we wanted to make it special. He loved watching the boats on the water. He ordered this pear and praline concoction. He was so little, and it was so big!" She laughed even as her eyes moistened with tears. "But he loved it so much, he ate it all."

Michelle knew the right thing to do. "We'll have a big slice of your Pear and Praline Cake." She spoke to the waitress but smiled at Paula, who looked at her with wide, grateful eyes. "And bring two forks."

Pears and pralines weren't Chocolate Truffle Cheesecake Delight, but this dessert tasted even sweeter when shared with a friend. Besides, Michelle consoled herself as she licked the last of it off her fork, she'd have the cheesecake next month when she came back to Branson to spend some time being there for an old friend.

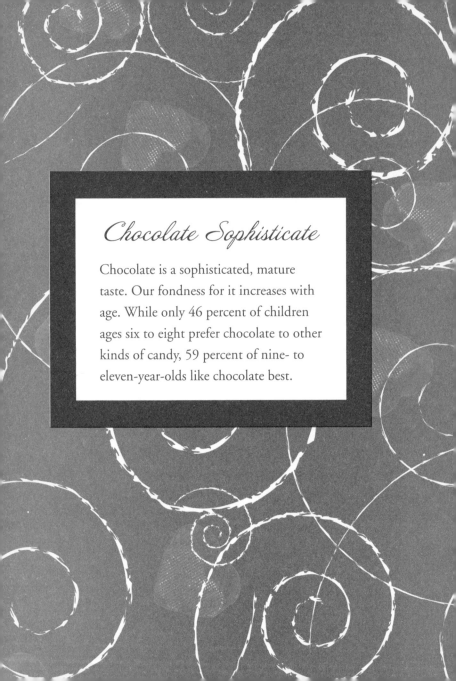

Chocolate Sophisticate

Chocolate is a sophisticated, mature taste. Our fondness for it increases with age. While only 46 percent of children ages six to eight prefer chocolate to other kinds of candy, 59 percent of nine- to eleven-year-olds like chocolate best.

Chapter 6
Sweet Refreshment

$\mathcal{A}$ friend's advice is refreshingly sweet to the heart. And as you refresh others, you'll experience My sweet refreshment. I will rejuvenate you when you're weary, and I'll satisfy you. Come to Me when you're stressed out, and you'll find rest for your soul. As you wait on and hope in Me, I'll renew your strength so you won't quit.

Reviving your soul,
Your God of Love
   —from Proverbs 27:9; 11:25;
   Jeremiah 31:25; Matthew 11:28–30;
   Isaiah 40:31

Nothing seems so refreshing as a delicious, cold drink on a hot summer day. Have you ever tried a chocolate Coke? It combines the refreshment of a cold drink with the special delight only chocolate can bring. Whether we eat it or drink it, chocolate releases seratonin in the brain, which causes feelings of pleasure and well-being. How's that for a re-freshing treat?

Did you know that while chocolate is an ancient food, dating back to the Mayan and Aztec civilizations in Central America, it was consumed only as a drink until the early Victorian era? That's when the process was developed for making chocolate solid. One Spanish conquistador wrote of seeing the Aztec ruler down fifty mugs of chocolate a day. Now that's sweet refreshment!

As refreshing as chocolate is, not even chocolate can rival the soul refreshment that comes from sweet friendship. Friends are like a breath of fresh air on a stagnant sea. They help us feel accepted, loved, safe, capable, and special. They share secrets, failures, and dreams for the future. Friends can buoy us up when we're sinking, urge us on when we hesitate, and applaud wildly as we approach some distant shore. Friends always make it worthwhile to return home again.

If you have a friend who refreshes your soul, you're fortunate. We all can strive to be such a friend—one who lifts another above the storms to a place of beauty and rest.

It is the sweet,
simple things of life which
are the real ones after all.

Laura Ingalls Wilder

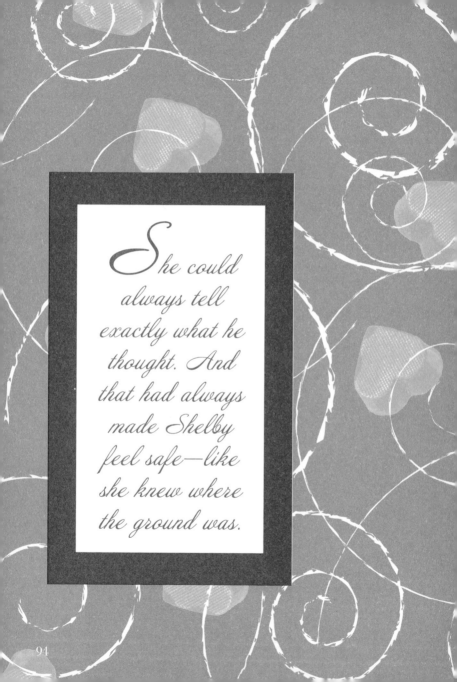

She could always tell exactly what he thought. And that had always made Shelby feel safe—like she knew where the ground was.

Bittersweet

Shelby took a long, deep breath as she strolled down the sidewalk of her old hometown. The late-morning October air was crisp and clear, and the sun was shining through the maple trees, most of which had lined historic Main Street—all five blocks of it—since before it was historic. The leaves were just reaching the brilliant shades of red and gold that blazed in peak season—a bit late this year because of the long, dry summer. She overheard locals commenting on the color.

"Didn't think we'd get much this year, with s' little rain."

"Yep. Guess that wave a storms came j'st in time to do some good."

Shelby smiled to hear the familiar small-town talk. It would be good to spend some time here, try to figure out her next move. She sighed. *I wish I believed it would all work out. No job, no ideas . . . what was I thinking?!*

Somewhere in the back of her mind, she had been

thinking that maybe she could retrace her steps, start over again—pursuing a dream instead of a goal. She'd met plenty of goals, and all they seemed to bring were stress, disillusionment, and a longing for some sense of peace. But where to find peace in a world like this? *What a silly notion, to think I could find it if I just went home again.*

She turned to head back toward a quaint little tearoom she'd noticed earlier, with chocolate scones in the display window. If she couldn't have peace, she could at least have the next best thing—chocolate. But just as she prepared to cross the street, a large, sweat-and-sawdust-covered construction worker backed into her, nearly knocking her into oncoming traffic (such as it was in Maple Ridge). Shelby recovered her balance and spun around to give this brute a piece of her mind when she realized he'd been backing out of an old building, carrying one end of a long countertop.

"Oops," he said in a strained voice. "'Scuse me."

The old marble slab must have weighed a ton. Still, he should watch where he's going.

"Sorry about that, ma'am. Gotta keep your eyes open with all this renovation goin' on."

"Me?!" Shelby couldn't believe he was blaming her for *his* carelessness. She threw him a half-mean, half-guilty look and kept going.

"Shelby?"

She turned and stared blankly at the man who had nearly knocked her over.

"Shelby Mathison?"

She forced a polite smile. "I'm sorry. Do I know you?"

He flashed a grin that made her stop and look hard. Something about those eyes when he smiled was familiar.

The stranger laughed. "Wanna get a chocolate Coke? I'll race you to the corner!"

Shelby gasped. "Kenny?!"

He blushed a little as his coworkers gave him sideways glances. "Most of the guys call me Ken."

"Of course—sorry. How in the world have you been? And what are you doing here? I thought your family moved to Idaho. What was that, sixth grade?"

He flashed that same easy smile. How could she have missed it the first time? Of course it was Kenny. Ken.

"Fifth grade, actually. We did, but I moved back here last year. My grandparents left me the house."

Shelby sucked in her breath. "That great old house on the hill? I remember; it was so beautiful with all those tall pines lining the driveway."

"That's the one. It needed some work, but it's given me something to do in my spare time, when I'm not here." He nodded toward the old storefront. "Hey, I'm just about ready to take off for lunch. Care to join me? We can catch up on old times."

"I'd love to!" *Ooh, Shelby, too eager.* She tried to hide the wince. They'd been best friends since kindergarten, until he'd moved away. *But he's grown up now, Shelby. He'll think*

you're flirting. Don't make a fool of yourself.

"Great! Give me just a few minutes, and I'll meet you at the deli." Ken wasn't hiding any of his enthusiasm. How could he still be so transparent? She could always tell exactly what he thought about everything. And somehow that had always made Shelby feel safe—like she knew where the ground was. How did he do that?

Shelby talked to herself the whole way to the deli. *Get a grip, Shelby. It's just a brief lunch to touch base. He has a whole separate life.* She felt a twinge in her stomach. *What if he's married? Of course he's probably married,* she scolded herself, *and what does it matter anyway? It's not like you're looking for a date. No more dates. Uh-uh.*

She slid into a corner booth. *But I sure could use a friend. A real friend, who doesn't have any ulterior motives.*

Stop it. What makes you think he wants to be friends again? For heaven's sake, Shelby, it's been twenty-five years. We're different people now. Besides, don't be so intense. Can't you be casual about anything?

The bell over the door jingled, and in walked Kenny—no, this was definitely Ken, and why hadn't she noticed he was so tall and good looking? *Stop it.*

She must have had a strange look on her face, because Ken's first words were, "Are you OK?"

"Huh? Oh, yeah—sorry. Lost in my thoughts. Nothing important, just baggage." *Shut up!* The last thing she wanted to do was talk about the ordeal in Chicago—and the fact that she was nowhere in her life. *Come on, Shelby, pull it together.*

He gave her a quizzical look. "Can I order you a sandwich?"

They ordered lunch and made small talk for a while, and Shelby relaxed again. "Remember how we used to sit at the soda shop and drink chocolate Cokes and talk about starting our own shop, with everything chocolate?"

Ken grinned and counted on his fingers. "Chocolate Cokes, of course, chocolate sodas and malts, about fifty flavors of chocolate ice cream, and every kind of chocolate fudge combination we could think of?"

Shelby smiled and wrinkled her nose. "I'm not sure the chocolate-tangerine mixture would have caught on." They laughed. "What was the name we had picked out for it again?" Shelby pretended to search her memory, but the truth was, she'd never forgotten. "Oh, I remember—The Chocolate Bar!"

Ken was looking into her eyes with a bemused smile, and Shelby realized she was enjoying this visit a little too much. She averted her gaze to hide the tears that suddenly were forming.

"Talk to me, Shelby. What's going on?"

"What do you mean?"

"I mean, I catch glimpses of you, but then you retreat again. What happened in Chicago?"

Shelby stared at him for a moment. "How did you know I was in Chicago?"

Ken blushed. "I—uh—your brother must have mentioned it, I guess."

Of course, Shelby, duh! "Oh, it's a long story."

"It's a small town, there's not much else to do," he said with a smirk.

Well, maybe I can just give him the summary version. Office politics, looking for new challenges, blah, blah.

An hour later, Shelby was stunned at how he made it so easy for her to bare her soul. How was that possible—with a man, first of all, and with this same guy after all these years? "So, long story made not short enough, I resigned in protest. Without a plan. I just left."

By now she'd become familiar with the raised-eyebrow look people got when she told her story and that now had come over Ken's face. It was the look that said she was truly psychotic and would probably end up broke and living in her parents' basement because she couldn't adapt to the politics of corporate life.

"I know, I know," she sighed. "It was idealistic, naive, and stupid." She fidgeted. "Wanna revisit that chocolate-shop idea?" She gave a weary, halfhearted chuckle.

Ken took a slow, deep breath.

Here it comes. The polite excuses. "Have to go, Shelby, and find someone who's not a raving lunatic."

"Actually, I was going to say I'm impressed. It took guts." He gave her foot a gentle kick under the table and smiled. "I guess the Shelby I knew is still in there after all."

Shelby shook her head ruefully. "I don't know."

"You'll see. She'll be back before you know it, stronger than ever."

Just then Shelby caught a glimpse of the clock on the wall. "Oh, my goodness! I didn't realize how long I'd rambled on. I'm so sorry. You must need to get back to work."

Ken's smile faded. "I guess I'd better get going." He got up to leave but turned around at the door. "Want to walk with me? I'll show you the project I'm working on."

"Your boss won't mind?"

"Huh? Oh—I'm the boss, I guess. It's just me and a few local guys, but we've restored some of the storefronts around here. This project is mine though. C'mon."

The leaves rustled pleasantly as they headed back to the construction site. As they stepped inside, she could see how careful his team was to preserve as much of the old material as possible.

"So you've been the one restoring all these old buildings? I've only been in a few, but they look fabulous!"

"Thanks. I didn't care much for my corporate job either." He pulled a dust cover off of some vintage stools as Shelby scanned the ornate ceiling tiles, exposed brick walls, and old signboards leaning against the base of the counter. She leaned her head sideways to read the old-fashioned, vertical sign similar to the ones other nearby shops had hung. She stared in disbelief as she read: The Chocolate Bar. She looked at Ken, who was leaning on a stool, watching her with that bemused look again.

He shrugged his shoulders. "I just thought maybe it'd be worth a shot. Actually, I had pretty much convinced myself it was a dumb idea and that I should sell the place when I was

finished with it." He took an unsteady breath. "And that's when I ran into you—uh, literally." He blushed and laughed nervously.

That's odd. I've never seen him nervous before.

"I know it sounds kind of hokey and naive," he said. "I just kind of thought maybe I'd come back and . . . I don't know . . . do something kind of peaceful. So maybe I'll keep it—if I can find the right partner."

Shelby smiled. "I know what you mean about wanting something peaceful. And I think I know someone who just might be interested."

Chocolate among the Nations

- Two countries salute chocolate on their national coats of arms. Fiji features a cocoa pod, and Ghana shows a cocoa tree.

- Switzerland consumes the most chocolate per capita, nearly twice that of the United States.

- Forty percent of cocoa beans come from Côte d'Ivoire (Ivory Coast) in West Africa, more than the next three producers combined.

- Chocolate lovers can visit chocolate museums in Barcelona, Spain; Quebec, Canada; Brussels, Belgium; Biarritz, France; Cologne, Germany; Birmingham, Alabama; and Chicago, Illinois.

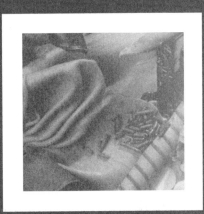

Chapter 7

Sweet Reassurance

*Y*ou can count on the love
of family and friends at all times.
When you feel the pressures of life
on all sides, you won't be crushed.
Although you're frustrated and don't
always understand why your life is
playing out the way it is, be assured
that I won't ever abandon you in the
midst of crisis. When you're knocked
down, I won't let you be destroyed.
I've marked you with the presence of
My spirit: it's My guarantee that I'll
fulfill all of My promises to you.

Encouraging you,
Your Faithful Friend and King
  —from Proverbs 17:17; 2 Corinthians 4:8–9;
  Ephesians 1:13–14

Turning cacao beans into chocolate is a long and difficult process. Cacao pods are hand sorted, crushed, and then roasted. Next the pods undergo winnowing, a grinding process that removes the hard outer hulls from the tender chocolate nibs. The chocolate is heated to a liquid through friction—the longer it endures the heat, or conching, the smoother and more refined its ultimate texture. The final stage is tempering, where the chocolate is cooled very carefully to attain the desired snap when broken, perfectly smooth meltability, and glossy shine. If the process is rushed, the chocolate will crystallize, ruining the finished product.

Life is a similar process. Families go through any number of difficult stages: crushing, winnowing, grinding, tempering, and refining. It's never pleasant to endure the protracted heat of conching or the delicate cooling required for tempering. But these stages are essential to producing the beautiful sheen and best quality in our families and in our lives.

Bearing the crushing or the heat isn't nearly as painful when families stick together. Indeed, it is these very processes that serve to blend families together in the most satisfying, long-lasting way.

If your family is being crushed in the crucible or feeling extreme heat, here's sweet reassurance: families that endure difficulties together stick together, love together, and eventually laugh together. Don't curse the blend-ing process embrace it—and your family.

The purpose of life, after all, is to live it, to taste experience to the utmost, to reach out eagerly and without fear for newer and richer experience.

Eleanor Roosevelt

They had both lost so much already. She couldn't bear to think of losing James too.

Staying Close

Maren Jensen felt almost as if she were home. The shop's little bell tinkled a light-hearted, familiar greeting as Maren stepped into the warmth of Johansen's Danish Pastry and Chocolate Shop. Her nose was delighted by the welcoming smells of assorted kringles, chocolate-filled rugelah, and fresh-baked Danish cookies she remembered from her childhood. Even the creak of the old wooden floor as she stomped snow from her boots brought back strong memories and feelings from childhood. She had spent many hours playing behind the counter in this shop as a little girl and, then as a teenager, many more helping to mix and bake the ableskiver—Danish desserts—and mold the chocolate candies.

She looked beyond the sweet treats in the glass display cases, hoping to glimpse a familiar face behind the counter. She was disappointed.

"May I help you?" asked a thin young woman, younger than Maren, perhaps even younger than James, Maren mused.

Sweet Reassurance

"Is Kamilla in today?" Maren asked hopefully. "Or Johann?"

"Ach!" Maren heard the familiar, guttural exclamation before she saw, emerging from the back room, a plump, sixtyish woman with her kinky blond—no, it was now white—hair pulled back neatly in a bun. The woman wiped her floured hands on her generous apron, producing a cloud that hung momentarily in the air. She looked at the one who had invoked her name. "Maren . . . Maren Jensen? Is that you? Ja, sure it is. You're the living image of your dear mother, more beautiful even than when I last saw you."

Maren was gratified to note the speed with which Kamilla moved around the counter to smother Maren in her ample bosom. It was another moment before she seemed to notice James, who stood shyly behind Maren. "And this must be your little brother, James," she gushed. She pulled him into her embrace without letting go of Maren. "Little? Look at you now. You're a man. And taller even than my own grandson Martin." She patted his cheek fondly. Maren could tell James was both pleased and embarrassed. It made him look younger than his eighteen years and made her ache at the thought of saying good-bye to him.

"We had to come one last time," Maren swallowed a lump rising in her throat. "James leaves for college Saturday . . ."

"I got a scholarship to MIT!" James chimed in excitedly.

"That's in Cambridge, Massachusetts," Maren added glumly. "It's 1,128.84 miles away." She had checked it at least a dozen times on MapQuest. She was absolutely sure of every single mile that would separate her from the little brother she had practically raised.

"Your mother would be so proud!" Kamilla exclaimed, clutching her hands to her chest dramatically. "If only she could have lived to see this day." She sniffled, then raised the hem of her large apron to dab at the corner of her eyes. "So you've come to say *farvel* to Kamilla and Johann."

"Of course," Maren assured her. "You and Johann are like family. If you hadn't taken Mama under your wing when she first came to America, given her a job and a familiar place to belong, I don't think we ever would have made it. We owe you so much. *Mange tak*. Many thanks."

"Besides," James seemed eager to break the emotional tension. "We were really hungry for the world's greatest chocolate-gilded sugar cones and chocolate sticks!"

Kamilla laughed appreciatively and tousled James's hair as she had done when he was little. He was still just a little boy, Maren observed wistfully. Would she be able to let him go, alone, so far from home, from everything familiar, from her?

Maren tried to smile as Kamilla filled a box with goodies at James's direction—and then another box—chocolate spritz cookies, marzipan, nut clusters, truffles, almond bark, chocolate kringle, Danish puffs, chocolate sticks, and other mouth-watering, fresh-baked treats she had loved as a child. It had been a difficult decision to leave this shop—and their familiar life in Milwaukee—after the sudden death of their mother. Maren had been nineteen and James just thirteen

when an aneurysm had first crippled, then killed, their beloved mother.

Their only living relative, a grandfather in Denmark, had pushed to have the children come live with him. But they had been born and raised in America. They barely knew their grandfather or the Danish language. Maren had resolved from the beginning that she would take care of James herself—no matter what.

At first she had thought she would leave the University of Wisconsin in Madison to return home to care for James. But she had thought better of delaying her studies and losing her generous scholarship. So James had moved to Madison with her, and they'd started a new life together.

She had done everything she could to provide for James, physically, financially, and emotionally. She didn't know much about mothering, except what she had observed from their mother—and Kamilla. Had it been enough to prepare James for the future? Had she given him all the skills he'd need to make it on his own, far from home? She wasn't convinced—not because of any lack in James, but in herself.

Maren had done everything she could to try to convince him to stay in Madison for school. She had even managed to get him to take his first semester at home. But he couldn't delay his scholarship at MIT any longer without losing it. He was determined to go. And she was having a difficult time letting him. They had both lost so much already. She couldn't bear to think of losing James too.

She was starting to better understand why it had felt important for her to bring him back here before he left for college. Down deep she hoped that their day of visiting the old places they'd enjoyed as children would awaken sentimental feelings of home and family in James. She hoped these feelings would anchor her brother's heart to home—to her—in spite of the distance that would soon come between them.

"*Uff da!*" Maren recognized Johann's voice above the tinkling bell and sound of rushing wind. He took off his gloves and turned down the collar on his overcoat as he furiously stomped his feet on the mat. "A storm's blowin' in for sure."

"Look, Johann! It's Maren and James!" Kamilla told her husband, who looked up for the first time.

"Maren!" He pecked her cheek with a warm, fatherly kiss. "James!" he grasped the boy firmly by the shoulders. Delight was evident in the rough features of his long, ruddy face. "Are you staying the night?"

"No, we've got to go. James leaves for college in two days."

"Then you've got to leave right now, or you won't make it." Johann spoke with an urgency that brought a stab of fear to Maren's heart.

After a hurried and emotional farewell, Maren and James loaded the chocolates into their old red Camry and headed toward the highway. Maren scanned the pewter-colored sky nervously. Flakes were already falling lightly. Would the storm hold off for the seventy minutes they needed to get home?

It had been a long, good day. James obviously didn't

share her worry. He chattered happily about his memories of the past. Maren smiled to realize that he hadn't once mentioned MIT.

After half an hour of talking, James had grown quiet and then fallen asleep. Deteriorating road conditions required Maren's total concentration. She could feel the tension in her neck and shoulders as she gripped the steering wheel.

She envied James his unworried sleep, even as she was grateful for his trust. She just hoped and prayed she'd be able to get them home in one piece. *Oh, why didn't we just stay the night? What should I do if it gets worse?*

Maren slowed to a crawl. The roads were practically deserted. Snow was piling up on the road, making driving difficult. The wind was whipping snow from the ground across the road, making it hard to see more than a few feet ahead. She couldn't see buildings or lights along the side of the road, couldn't even make out the lanes or edges of the road. The beams from her headlights were swallowed by the storm just beyond the hood. It took her twenty minutes to go only five miles. At this rate, it would take two more hours to get home—if she could get there at all. Maren felt panic starting to rise in her heart. What should she do?

Suddenly something large roared by in the next lane. She could feel it shaking her car and kicking up snow. At first it terrified her and made her feel like she was going to crash. But then she realized it was a snowplow. She could just see its taillights disappearing into the swirl in front of her. Without hesitating, Maren changed lanes, stepped on the gas, and hurried to catch up. The road was remarkably clear behind the plow. And although she still couldn't see through the snow, as long as she kept her eyes on those taillights, she could follow with no problem. They were going seventy miles per hour. At this rate, they'd be home in about twenty minutes.

For the first time in almost an hour, Maren felt she was going to make it. She relaxed her grip on the wheel and leaned back into the seat. She looked over at her brother and was surprised to realize that he'd been watching her intently. She smiled at him.

"You've done a great job, sis," he said quietly.

"We're not home yet."

"That isn't what I'm talking about." He rested his hand meaningfully on her leg. "*Mange mange tak*."

"*Selv tak*," Maren thanked him back, her eyes misting with tears.

"I know it's hard to say good-bye. Neither of us can see the future. But I can promise that my road will always lead me back to you—to all that we've shared. I'll never forget our heritage. You've been a great example."

They both fell silent. Maren didn't know what to say, but she savored the happy feeling in her heart.

Suddenly the lights in front of her slowed and blinked. Maren watched carefully, unsure what was happening. The plow's right turn signal flashed, then stopped. Maren noticed the snow-covered sign announcing the Madison exit. The

plow then roared off down the highway. Maren flashed her high beams to try to communicate thanks to her mysterious benefactor. She'd have to navigate the last few miles on her own. But it wasn't far now, and Maren felt confident she could make it.

Then it occurred to her: the snowplow had cleared her path and lighted her way for the hardest part of her journey, just as she had cleared the path for James. It was time for him to continue on his own. But now Maren felt more confident. She'd done a good job. James was going to make it on his own. And so was she.